PRAISE F

BROKEN CRAYONS STILL COLOR

Broken Crayons Still Color is a book of healing and hope. Full of wisdom, encouragement, and stories, its words show us over and over again our God who mends our hearts and restores our wholeness. Come alongside Shelley as she shares her story and you will find strength and nourishment for your own story.

> Jean Wise, Writer, Speaker, Retreat Leader, and Spiritual Director
> www.healthyspirituality.org

Gorgeous. This book is a work of art. The words, the feelings, the questions, the art within the book. Shelley, thank you for your brave vulnerability as you help each of us see how miraculous we are! God loves us so much. He wants us to keep coloring.

> Diane Cunningham, Coach, Author, Life Artist, www.dianecunningham.com

As a Christian Counselor, I can see so many ways the *Broken Crayons Still Color* products can be used in the lives of the people we counsel. The videos, the skillfully written and heartfelt prayers and words, the viewer's guide and next steps, the coloring pages, and the reflection questions will gently touch participants on various levels using all senses!

It's hard to find a book about brokenness that so completely points those who are hurting to the Redeemer and gives them blessed hope. I so appreciate Shelley's vulnerability and honesty in sharing and her willingness to let Christ fill her life with Himself!

> Karen Lindwall-Bourg, MA, LPC-Supervisor, www.rhemacounseling.com

Shelley Hitz is an outstanding writer with a gift from God to help you experience God through the creativity of coloring. Through her own story of brokenness, healing, and deliverance, Shelley takes you through on a journey to help you start the process of healing, and letting go of the past. *Broken Crayons Still Color* will increase your faith and give you confidence in knowing that regardless of what you've gone through, God loves you and will take the pain of your past and use it for his glory. The coloring pages and interactive activities will help you dive deeper into the word of God, help you apply the word to your life, and provides you with an opportunity to reflect on God's grace, mercy, and forgiveness.

> Dr. LaWanda N. Evans, Licensed Professional Counselor, National Certified Counselor,
> The Healthy Relationship Institute, www.drlne.com

BROKEN CRAYONS
STILL COLOR

FROM OUR MESS TO GOD'S MASTERPIECE

Shelley Hitz

Body and Soul Publishing LLC

COLORADO SPRINGS, COLORADO

Shelley Hitz
P.O. Box 6542
Colorado Springs, CO 80934
www.ShelleyHitz.com

Book Layout ©2013 Book Design Templates
www.shelleyhitz.com/booktemplates

Broken Crayons Still Color / Shelley Hitz, 1st Edition

ISBN-10: 1-946118-01-X
ISBN-13: 978-1-946118-01-1

Book cover image credit Molly McMillan, http://mollymcmillan.com
Edited by Deb Hall, http://thewriteinsight.com

All scripture quotations, unless otherwise indicated, are taken from the Holy Bible, New International Version®, NIV®. Copyright © 1973, 1978, 1984, 2011 by Biblica, Inc.□ Used by permission of Zondervan. All rights reserved worldwide, www.zondervan.com. The "NIV" and "New International Version" are trademarks registered in the United States Patent and Trademark office by Biblica, Inc.□

Scripture marked (KJV) are taken from the King James Version, public domain.

Scripture marked (NKJV) are taken from the New King James Version®. Copyright © 1982 by Thomas Nelson. Used by permission. All rights reserved.

Scripture quotations marked (AMP) are taken from the Amplified Bible, Copyright © 1954, 1958, 1962, 1964, 1965, 1987 by The Lockman Foundation. Used by permission.

Scripture quotations marked (AMPC) are taken from the Amplified® Bible (AMPC), Copyright © 1954, 1958, 1962, 1964, 1965, 1987 by The Lockman Foundation. Used by permission. www.Lockman.org

Scripture quotations marked (ESV) are from the ESV® Bible (The Holy Bible, English Standard Version®), copyright © 2001 by Crossway, a publishing ministry of Good News Publishers. Used by permission. All rights reserved.

Scripture quotations marked (NASB) are taken from the New American Standard Bible® (NASB), Copyright © 1960, 1962, 1963, 1968, 1971, 1972, 1973, 1975, 1977, 1995 by The Lockman Foundation. Used by permission. www.Lockman.org.

Bonus Material:

Download the bonus material that corresponds with this book (coloring pages, scripture cards, etc.) here: http://www.brokencrayonsbook.com

CONTENTS

How to Use This Book

Let me be honest with you for a moment.

I did not want to write this book. That's right. I put off writing this book for almost a year.

I remember very clearly standing in my sister's church on June 19, 2016, and although I did not hear an audible voice, God made it very clear to me I was to finish this project.

Being vulnerable and real, I share my own story of moving from my messes to God's masterpiece inside this book. And believe me, I am still a work in progress.

I share my story in order to encourage you and bring glory to God. Revelation 12:11 says,

> They triumphed over him (Satan)
> by the blood of the Lamb
> and by the word of their testimony.

When we share the testimony of how God brought healing and freedom into our lives, we overcome the enemy.

In Each Chapter

Each chapter will have its own theme as well as a theme color. I will share stories and illustrations to help you apply the concepts of each theme to your life.

I wanted to do something different with this book that would engage our right brains and our emotions as we apply the Bible to our lives.

Therefore, I have coloring pages for each chapter and reflection questions for you to pray about and meditate on while you color. These can also be used as journaling prompts to write out in a separate journal. It's up to you.

This is completely optional, but I encourage you to try it!

I have found that as an adult I have neglected the creative side of my brain for a long time. When I get out my markers, colored pencils, or crayons and begin doodling, painting, or coloring, there is something that comes alive within me.

I have also included a theme verse for each chapter that you can memorize and meditate on throughout the week.

If you want to go even deeper, I have included a corresponding video with each chapter that includes a fill-in-the blank Viewer's Guide. You can go through this on your own or use it in a group.

If you use this book in a group, there is a Leader's Guide with discussion questions in the Appendix to help you get the most out of this book study.

Are you ready to dive in?

Let's do this!

Introduction

Tears were streaming down my face until I could not see clearly enough to drive.

I decided to pull over to the side of the road to gain my composure. As soon as I put my car in park, the sobs came fast and furious. I wondered if they would ever stop.

However, I slowly felt the weight of regret and shame I had been living with for years begin to lift. My shoulders relaxed as I wiped the tears from my eyes.

In the background I could still hear the lyrics of the song that triggered this emotional response.

History. My sins are history.

But did I really believe it?

God was about to teach me a powerful lesson that would change the direction of my life forever.

Broken Crayons

Recently, when visiting my nieces in Florida, I got down on the floor to color with them. They love the Disney princesses, and so we were coloring a picture of Cinderella.

When we opened their container of crayons, a burst of colors greeted us.

These were well-worn crayons that had been used to color dozens of pictures.

I chose a broken and worn-out green crayon.

In our throwaway society, it would be easy to think that the work of this crayon was done. That it needed to be replaced with a brand-new crayon instead.

However, as I began to color with this broken worn-out crayon, my nieces looked at me and told me my coloring page was beautiful.

Because, you see, broken crayons still color.

Our Brokenness

Just like that broken worn-out crayon, we can also feel useless to God because of the mistakes we have made or the things that have been done to us.

We feel broken and ugly and useless.

We think God would rather have someone else do His work. Someone with less brokenness and baggage. Someone who has it all together.

The truth is, we all have brokenness in our lives. Many times we compare our blooper reel to someone else's highlight reel.

The truth is no one has a perfect life.

And just like that broken crayon, God is always able to use our brokenness to create something beautiful.

A masterpiece.

It reminds me of the story of the broken pot often told in India. The author is unknown, but the story is powerful.

This story describes my life so well, as God has chosen to use my brokenness and the healing He has brought into my life to create something beautiful.

> There was a water bearer in India who had two large pots. Each hung on the ends of a pole that he carried across the back of his neck. One of the pots had a small crack in it near the bottom. The other pot was perfect and always delivered a full portion of water at the end of the long walk from the stream to the master's house, but the pot that was broken arrived only half full.
>
> For two years this went on daily, with the bearer delivering only one and a half pots full of water to his master's house. Of course, the perfect pot was proud of its accomplishments, bragging constantly about its full measure of water when it arrived. But the poor broken pot was ashamed of its imperfection and miserable

that it was able to retain only half of what it was supposed to hold. After two years of what the cracked pot perceived as a bitter failure, it spoke to the water bearer one day by the stream.

"I am ashamed of myself, and I want to apologize to you."

"Why?" asked the bearer. "What are you ashamed of?"

"I have been able, for these past two years, to carry only half my load because this crack that I am afflicted with causes water to leak out all the way back to your master's house. Because of my flaws, you have to do all of this work, and you don't get full value from your efforts," the pot said.

The water bearer felt sorry for the poor broken pot, and in his compassion he said, "As we return to the master's house, I want you to notice the beautiful flowers along the path."

As they went up the hill, the old pot noticed the sun warming some beautiful wildflowers on the side of the path, and this cheered the pot a little. But at the end of the trail, it still felt bad because it had leaked out half its load, and so again it apologized to the bearer for its failure.

The bearer said to the pot, "Did you notice that there were flowers only on your side of your path, but not on the other pot's side? That's because I have always known about your flaw, and I took advantage of it. I planted flower seeds on your side of the path, and every day while we walk back from the stream, you've watered them. For two years I have been able to pick these beautiful flowers to decorate my master's table. Without you being just the way you are, my master would not have this beauty to grace his house."

—Author Unknown[1]

Many times what we see as our biggest mistakes and failures can become what God uses the most.

However, the enemy in our minds often tells us we are worthless and no longer useful for God's kingdom.

Little do we know that God is using our brokenness to create something more beautiful than we could ever imagine.

It's Time to Color!

As you begin to consider your own brokenness, seek to hear from God. Ask Him for His Spirit to wash over you as you color.

Download printable coloring pages from this book here:
www.brokencrayonsbook.com

Reflection Questions:

While you color, I encourage you to reflect, pray, and meditate on these questions. You can also use them as journaling prompts in a separate journal of your own.

1. Do I see myself as the broken pot in the story? If so, how?
2. Do I see others' brokenness and judge them based on their past mistakes?
3. Pray and ask God to help you see yourself as God sees you and see others as He sees them.

Prayer

Lord, thank you that you never waste anything that has happened in our lives. I thank you that you can turn my brokenness into something beautiful even when I cannot see it.

Help me to open my heart to you and allow you to bring healing and freedom.

I love you.

In Jesus' name I pray, amen.

Hide His Word in Your Heart

For each chapter, I have also provided a Scripture memory verse for you to go deeper.

This week's memory verse is Isaiah 61:1:

> *The Spirit of the Sovereign Lord is on me,*
> *because the Lord has anointed me*
> *to proclaim good news to the poor.*
> *He has sent me to bind up the brokenhearted,*
> *to proclaim freedom for the captives*
> *and release from darkness for the prisoners.*

Here are several ways you can meditate on each week's memory verse:

1. Write out this week's verse on an index card and carry it with you.
2. Set up a daily reminder on your mobile device to review the verse.
3. Consider changing your screen saver to this week's verse.
4. Write the verse on your mirror with a dry erase marker.
5. Post the verse around your home with sticky notes.
6. Print off the Scripture cards I have had my designer create for you and have them laminated. Download them here: www.brokencrayonsbook.com

Going Deeper

For each chapter, I have created a corresponding video teaching. You can use the video, viewer's guide, and discussion questions in a group or you can go through them on your own. The leader's guide can be found in the back of this book.

Watch the Introduction video here:
www.brokencrayonsbook.com/video-intro

Introduction
Viewer's Guide

The Spirit of the Sovereign Lord is on me, because the Lord has anointed me to proclaim good news to the poor. He has sent me to bind up the brokenhearted, to proclaim freedom for the captives and release from darkness for the prisoners.

—Isaiah 61:1

Forgiveness = _____

There is often stuff in our lives that _____ our relationship with God.

Those clogs are often _____, the ways we've missed God's mark and His standard for our lives.

"He is faithful and just . . . will forgive our sins . . . and _____ from _____ unrighteousness" (1 John 1:9 AMP).

Forgiveness = the _____ to Freedom

The Forgiveness Cross

Asking _____

2 Corinthians 5:10, Hebrews 9:27–28

"If you, Lord, kept a record of sins, who could stand? But with you _____, so that we can, with reverence, serve you" (Ps. 130:3–4).

God puts our sins in his ocean of grace and forgiveness and puts a sign up that says, "_____." (Hebrews 10:17)

Profession of Faith Prayer

There is no "magic prayer" for salvation. However, I want to share the following simple prayer you can use if you want to make a profession of faith:

> Lord, I admit I'm a sinner, and I now put my faith in you alone and what you accomplished for me both by dying on the cross and by being raised to life. I surrender my life into your hands, and I make you Lord over every area of my life. I ask that you would fill me with your Holy Spirit. Lead and guide my life from this day forward. I ask this in Jesus' name, amen.

If you made a profession of faith, I encourage you to get a Bible, find a church that teaches from the Bible, and ask someone who is a mature Christian any questions you may have.

Our Broken Pieces

God can take our _____ pieces and create a _____.

I am a _____.

Your Next Steps

1. Memorize this week's theme verse.
2. Use the reflection questions in the Introduction.
3. Read Chapter One

Chapter One:

~~The Ugliness of Sin~~ The Beauty of Grace and Forgiveness

Entering April 2016 marked twenty-four years of following Christ in my life. I was blessed to grow up in a Christian home and was baptized when I was seven, but I did not choose to fully surrender my life to Christ until my junior year in high school.

Once I committed my life to Christ, I figured everything in my life would be perfect from that point on. How wrong I was. Sometimes we get the idea that being a Christian excludes us from certain trials, hardships, and pain, but the Bible tells us differently.

In John 16:33 Jesus says,

> In this world you will have trouble. But take heart! I have overcome the world.

Notice Jesus doesn't say you might have trouble or if you have enough faith you won't have trouble . . . He says you will have trouble.

Even though I was a Christian, I experienced a great deal of brokenness and pain.

My grandma was murdered when I was eight years old, I experienced an instance of sexual abuse in junior high school, and my dad was emotionally unavailable for me as I grew up. My life was not perfect in the least, but I still tried to create the image that I had it all together.

My Secret Sin

The darkest time in my life started, however, when I was twenty-five years old and had been married two years. My husband, CJ, was in full-time ministry with Youth for Christ, and I was very involved in our church. To the outside world, I looked like I had it all together. I was the "good girl."

However, even "good girls" fall.

And fall I did.

I fell into an intense battle with a secret sin, an addiction to Internet pornography, which lasted for two years.

How could this happen?

I even shocked myself. I couldn't believe I was doing it, and yet I couldn't seem to stop.

Looking back, I can see that the main trigger to my porn addiction was loneliness. I was most vulnerable when CJ was gone for a week at a time at a youth event or training. Not only was I lonely and longing for emotional intimacy when CJ was gone, but I was also home alone.

As you probably know, an addiction to pornography thrives in secrecy. Therefore, it was something I could easily hide from CJ when he was away.

I Realized I Needed Help

I knew I was on a road to destruction that could eventually destroy my intimacy with God and destroy my marriage if nothing changed.

I am so thankful God gave me the courage at that time to reach out for help. I confessed my sin both to God and to my husband. I also started Christian counseling. I would love to say I never gave in to viewing pornography after that point. But it didn't happen that way.

As with most people who struggle with sexual addiction, it took time. I would take two steps forward and then one step back.

Through God's grace, I am free today.

God Works in Mysterious Ways

It is often said that God works in mysterious ways.

On that fate-filled day when I sat in my car with tears streaming down my cheeks, God worked a miracle in my heart.

I was not in church; I was not in a prayer meeting; I was not even aware of the bondage I was in at the time.

But God, in His mercy and grace, reached down to me that day.

I was listening to Christian radio and the song "History" by Matthew West began to play.

As I listened to the words of that song, the Holy Spirit began to speak to my heart.

Although I had asked for God's forgiveness and truly repented of my sin, I was still living in the bondage of regret and shame.

I had sensed God leading me into ministry for teen girls, but I did not think God could use me.

I knew what I was doing. I chose to sin even though I knew it was wrong.

I did it anyway.

And the thoughts in my mind tormented me. I would hear thoughts like "Stupid, stupid, stupid! You knew better, how could you?"

I cannot fully explain what happened that day on the side of the road, but I know part of it was being able to forgive myself.

Just as we are to forgive others their sins against us, I believe we may also need to forgive ourselves. And a big part of that is accepting God's complete forgiveness of our sins.

Yes, we do need to confess our sin to Christ. That's the first step.

However, I had already taken that step. Not only did I confess my sin, but I had truly repented. Repentance means to turn away from your sin and start going in the opposite direction.

I was no longer actively involved in pornography. I went to counseling and got help, I had an accountability partner, I put filters on my computer, and God had empowered me to truly change.

But I still saw myself as dirty and broken.

All I could think about was the mistakes I had made and how I wished I could go back and make better decisions. Different decisions.

I often had haunting thoughts that began with "If only."

My regret ran deep and held me captive.

However, God wanted to use my brokenness for His glory.

He wanted me to know that I was completely forgiven!

The old Shelley was gone. I was a new creation.

If I would allow Him, God would begin to paint a beautiful masterpiece with the brokenness of my life.

Years later I was in a Bible study where God used the words of Zechariah to bring an even deeper healing within me.

Zechariah 3:1–5 (NKJV) says,

> Then he showed me Joshua the high priest standing before the Angel of the Lord, and Satan standing at his right hand to oppose him. And the Lord said to Satan, "The Lord rebuke you, Satan! The Lord who has chosen Jerusalem rebuke you! Is this not a brand plucked from the fire?"
>
> Now Joshua was clothed with filthy garments, and was standing before the Angel.
>
> Then He answered and spoke to those who stood before Him, saying, "Take away the filthy garments from him." And to him He said, "See, I have removed your iniquity from you, and I will clothe you with rich robes."
>
> And I said, "Let them put a clean turban on his head."
>
> So they put a clean turban on his head, and they put the clothes on him. And the Angel of the Lord stood by.

I saw myself standing before the Lord in my filthy garments. I thought my identity would be tied to those filthy garments forever. However, Christ took those garments from me, removed my iniquity, and clothed me with His robes of righteousness.

This Scripture shows us that Christ rebukes Satan for us. He is for us, not against us.

And He wants to do the same for you.

Are you living with the heavy weight of shame and regret from your past?

Do you feel that God could never use you because of what you have done or the things that have been done to you?

If so, the first step is forgiveness.

When I was in counseling, I learned about the forgiveness cross.

The Forgiveness Cross

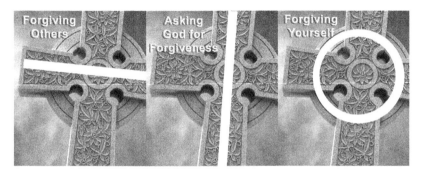

Image source: Bob Smith, "Stone Cross," FreeImages.com, accessed September 7, 2016

The horizontal part of the cross is forgiving others, the vertical part is asking God for His forgiveness of our sin, and the circle in the middle is forgiving ourselves.

I had forgiven those who sexually abused me, I had asked God for his forgiveness, and I had repented of my sin. But there was one step left.

That day while I was driving, I distinctly sensed God saying to me in my heart, "Shelley, you've forgiven others, but you haven't forgiven yourself. It's time to let go of this regret and forgive yourself."

As I said, I had to pull over to the side of the road because I was crying so hard.

It was true.

I needed to forgive myself.

And as I did, a weight was lifted off of me. I was forgiven and I could move on.

Shortly after, God used me to launch a ministry for teen girls that has impacted thousands of girls around the world and still continues today.

You see, broken crayons still color.

It's Time to Color!

If you have deep wounds from the past, I recommend consulting a pastor, Christian counselor, or someone you can trust to help you walk through the steps of healing.

Before you begin coloring, you may want to pray a prayer of surrender. If so, you can pray something like this:

> Lord, I want to be free from anything that weighs me down and the sin that so easily entangles me (Heb. 12:1–2). I surrender to you my heart, mind, and will, and I ask that you lead me through this time of journaling and prayer. Help me to be willing to deal with any sin in my life that keeps me from you and hinders my spiritual growth. I acknowledge your power to forgive any sin and to help me do what I cannot do on my own. In Jesus' name I pray, amen.

Download printable coloring pages from this book here: www.brokencrayonsbook.com

Reflection Questions:

While you color, I encourage you to reflect, pray, and meditate on these questions:

1. Is there any unconfessed sin that I need to bring to God today? If something comes to mind, stop and confess it to God right now.
2. Is there someone who has deeply hurt me whom I need to forgive through the power of Christ? If so, ask for God's help to walk through the steps of forgiveness. My book Forgiveness Formula may help you as you walk through the process.
3. Am I still weighed down with shame and regret from my past mistakes? What are the areas that I need to forgive myself and truly accept Christ's forgiveness for my sins? If there is something in particular that comes to mind, ask God to help you let go of the shame and regret and live instead in His righteousness.

THE *Beauty* OF

grace

Prayer

Once you are ready, you can pray a prayer asking God for forgiveness of your sins. There is no "magic prayer," but you can choose to use the following prayer as an example.

> Lord, I confess and repent of my sin(s) of _____. I ask you to forgive me, and I receive your forgiveness. I forgive myself for participating in this sin.
>
> I ask for the empowerment of the Holy Spirit to help me truly repent of my sin(s) of _____ and help me to change direction. Please show me how I need to change and help me, Holy Spirit, to make those changes despite what my friends and family may think or say. Thank you for taking the weight of this sin from me and restoring my relationship with you.
>
> In Jesus' name I pray, amen.

Write out any changes you sense God asking you to make as you repent of your sin(s). I recommend that you find an accountability partner to help you and pray for you as you make these changes.

Hide His Word in Your Heart

This week's memory verse is 2 Corinthians 5:17:

> *Therefore, if anyone is in Christ, the new creation has come: The old has gone, the new is here!*

Going Deeper

Watch the video for Chapter One here:
www.brokencrayonsbook.com/video-one

Chapter One
Viewer's Guide

Therefore, if anyone is in Christ, the new creation has come.
The old has gone, the new is here!
—2 Corinthians 5:17

Forgiveness of others is often the _____ we take when healing from hurts in our lives.

The _____ of Unforgiveness

"If you have anything against anyone, forgive him and _____ (drop the issue, let it go), so that your Father who is in heaven will also forgive you your transgressions and wrongdoings [against Him and others]. [But if you do not forgive, neither will your Father in heaven forgive your transgressions" (Mark 11:25–26 AMPC).

It took me time to truly forgive from _____ (Matt. 18:35).

Jesus showed us by example how to forgive: "Father, _____, for they know not what they do" (Luke 23:34 ESV).

Repentance (Luke 15:7)

Why Do We Need to Forgive Ourselves?

Sometimes although we've repented and God's forgiven us, we still have _____ for our mistakes and sins of the past.

However, we are to love our neighbor as we love _____ (Matt. 22:39).

The Forgiveness Cross

1) Forgiving _____

2) Asking _____ for forgiveness

3) Forgiving _____

What do you need to put in _____?

Your Next Steps

1. Memorize this week's theme verse.
2. Use the reflection questions in Chapter One.
3. Read Chapter Two.

Chapter Two:
~~Used and Abused~~ Valuable and Loved

I t was 2007 and I was about to experience another life-changing moment of healing that I believe came directly from the hand of God.

You know those moments in time.

The ones you will never forget because of the deep, deep healing and freedom that came as a result.

I was at a women's retreat in Ohio, and the speaker was sharing her testimony. She talked openly about an instance of sexual abuse that was "just touching" but very painful and hurtful to her. She talked about her healing process and how God freed her from the pain.

That day, as she talked, something she said struck a raw nerve inside of me. It was as if for the first time I was given permission to grieve what had been taken from me the day I was abused. My innocence. My trust.

It was wrong and I had been violated.

They gave us time to go off by ourselves on the retreat grounds to process the session. During my time alone, I cried and cried. They were cleansing tears helping me to grieve what happened to me over twenty years ago.

I always thought that the incident was "no big deal" and that it was a normal part of growing up. I would compare what happened to me to the intense abuse some people walk through and simply dismiss it. I swept it under the rug of my heart and moved on.

But you know what I realized that day?

I realized that it was a big deal to me. It had deeply wounded me, more than I realized, and I needed to heal from it.

You see, I experienced an incident of sexual abuse when I was in eighth grade. I did not recognize it as sexual abuse or even grieve what happened to me until I was at that retreat center sitting in the grass by myself.

With God's empowerment, I began a healing process. It started with grieving my loss and feeling the pain. I then realized it was time to forgive the boy who sexually abused me, which was difficult.

I felt angry with him because he forced himself upon me and stole my innocence and purity that day. This one moment in time distorted my view of sex and led me down a path of brokenness and pain related to my sexuality.

I take full responsibility for my actions, but I believe there is a connection between this incident of sexual abuse and my addiction to pornography. In fact, a majority of the women I talk to who struggle with a pornography addiction also have been sexually abused in their past. It seems to be a common thread.

Because of the deep impact the sexual abuse had on my life, my anger ran deep and it was difficult to forgive. It took time and the empowerment of the Holy Spirit to finally let go of my resentment and unforgiveness.

One day while I was praying, several months after the retreat, I asked God where He was during that difficult time.

Note: if you have experienced severe abuse in the past and want to use the type of prayer I describe below—often called inner healing prayer—I recommend that you seek outside help from a pastor or Christian counselor and not go through this process alone. It can often be a very intense emotional experience and can even trigger PTSD if the abuse was severe.

In my time of prayer, I saw myself on a charter bus with my eighth-grade class on the way home from a field trip. I was sitting next to a good-looking guy I had a huge crush on at the time. It was on that bus, under a blanket, that he did things to me I never wanted.

I did not know how to say no or even what to do. I simply let it happen. At that point in my life, I was innocent. I had not even kissed a boy before, let alone experience what happened to me that night.

The picture I got during prayer was of the guy on the bus taking a knife and stabbing my "heart." It was as if my heart was made of glass and shattered into a million pieces the day the sexual abuse occurred. It was not my physical heart that was damaged, but my inner heart and emotions.

However, I saw Jesus standing there crying and then lovingly picking up every last piece of my heart.

He showed me the pieces and then said, "You aren't ready for them now, but I'll keep them safe for you." I then saw Him put all the pieces of my heart into a safe and lock it with a key.

He said to me, "Shelley, you've looked to your husband and to many other things to heal your heart, but I'm the only one who has the key."

Then He looked at me and said, "*Now* you're ready."

I saw Jesus take out my broken heart from the safe; He was holding all the pieces in His hands. Right before my eyes, my heart was miraculously restored and all the broken pieces came back together to form a complete heart. He placed my restored heart back in my chest, but it was still not fully functioning and alive. I then watched Him give me CPR compressions to get the blood flowing back through my heart again. The blood represented the Holy Spirit, which flows in and through my restored heart.

I can't fully explain it with words, but from somewhere deep inside I finally felt whole again.

It was a process of healing that started at the retreat and took place over time.

The next week in church we sang the song, based on the verse from Mark 12:30, "Love the Lord your God with all your heart and with all your soul and with all your mind and with all your strength."

I sensed God saying to me, "Shelley, now you can love me with *all* your heart!"

Tears streamed down my cheeks because I knew a deep healing had taken place.

I was free. My broken heart was made whole again. Like a mosaic of broken pieces glued together to create a beautiful piece of art, God brought healing to my broken pieces.

Just like the broken pieces of a crayon cannot be brought back together but instead can be melted into something new, my broken pieces were made into something new that day. And yours can too.

I still have the emotional scars. However, a deep healing took place in my heart.

You see, broken crayons do still color.

God is the artist and our lives are His canvas.

What will you allow Him to create from the broken pieces in your life?

It's Time to Color!

As you begin to consider your own brokenness, seek to hear from God. Ask Him for His Spirit to wash over you as you color.

Download printable coloring pages from this book here:
www.brokencrayonsbook.com

Reflection Questions:

If you have deep wounds from the past, I recommend consulting a pastor, Christian counselor, or someone you can trust to help you walk through the steps.

While you color, I encourage you to reflect, pray, and meditate on these questions:

1. What stuck out from Shelley's story to me in this chapter? Did it stir any emotions within me?
2. Are there any wounds from my past that need healing? If so, am I ready and willing to begin the healing process with the help of God?
3. Is there anyone I need to forgive from my past?
4. Jesus is the only one able to bring healing to my broken heart. What does that statement mean to me? Do I believe it to be true for me?
5. What is God saying to me today regarding my own wounds from the past?

Prayer

Lord, thank you that you are able to bring healing to the brokenhearted and set the captives free. Thank you that no matter what has been done to me in the past, healing is possible. Thank you for all that you have revealed to me through this chapter, and I surrender my brokenness to you today for healing.

I rest today in the promise that NOTHING can separate me from your love. I am loved by you and can rest in that love today. In Jesus' name I pray, amen.

Hide His Word in Your Heart

This week's memory verse is Romans 8:38–39:

> For I am convinced that neither death nor life, neither angels nor demons, neither the present nor the future, nor any powers, neither height nor depth, nor anything else in all creation, will be able to separate us from the love of God that is in Christ Jesus our Lord.

Going Deeper

Watch the video for Chapter Two here:
www.brokencrayonsbook.com/video-two

Chapter Two
Viewer's Guide

For I am convinced that neither death nor life, neither angels nor
demons, neither the present nor the future, nor any powers, neither
height nor depth, nor anything else in all creation, will be able to
separate us from the love of God that is in Christ Jesus our Lord.
—Romans 8:38–39

There is _____.

2 Corinthians 10:3–4

Sometimes we need to go deeper to get to the _____.

"There are no _____ with God. The way in which God heals
our wounds is a deeply personal process. He is a person and He insists
on working personally." —John Eldredge[1]

Healing is _____.

Luke 4:18–19, Matthew 12:20, Matthew 8:7, Matthew 4:23, Luke 6:19,
Luke 9:11, Matthew 8:16

_____ with God is key.

The words of Joseph:

> *"You intended to harm me, but God intended it for good to accomplish what is now being done, the saving of many lives."* (Gen. 50:20)

Healing starts with a _____ heart.

Prayer of Surrender

> Lord, I surrender to you my heart, mind, and will and ask that you lead me through this journey to healing and freedom. Help me to be willing to deal with the issues of my past that are hindering my spiritual growth. I acknowledge your power to overcome any obstacle standing in my way and your ability to help me do what I cannot do myself. Empower me to change through your Holy Spirit. Amen.

Your Next Steps

1. Memorize this week's theme verse.
2. Use the reflection questions in Chapter Two.
3. Read Chapter Three.

Book referenced in the video can be found in the resources section of the Appendix.

Chapter Three:

~~Body Image Imperfections~~ Fearfully and Wonderfully Made

Body image issues are so common in our culture today. A majority of teen girls and women I talk to struggle with body image. Even men feel the pressure to look a certain way.

Here is one body image lie we often believe:

If I can change _____ (fill in the blank) about my body, others will finally accept me and I will be able to accept myself.

It is so easy to base our worth on our outward appearance because it is the first thing others see.

As I started to work on this area in my life, I realized one day that I was addicted to mirrors. I was always checking my appearance to see if I looked okay. Some days I would feel good about what I saw because my hair or outfit looked cute. However, other days I simply wanted to go home and hide due to a new acne breakout.

I was on a roller coaster of emotions based on how I looked each day. Perfection was my goal. Therefore, I was never happy with the way I looked.

What Would You Change About Your Body?

If you could change one thing about your physical appearance, what would it be?

I know my answer without even thinking about it. I bet most of you already know your answer too. The thing I have struggled with the most is acne and the scars it has left behind.

In high school I had a perfect complexion. I even remember someone commenting that my skin looked like a china doll. Well, that soon ended when I entered college.

I am not even sure what caused it. My best guess: a combination of bad eating habits and hormones. I thought it would just be a short phase and then be gone. But it lasted into my thirties, and even now in my forties I still struggle with occasional acne breakouts.

UUUGGGGHHHH!!

I tried most everything from Mary Kay to Proactiv to Arbonne to supplements and vitamins to hormone creams, changing my diet, etc.

Nothing worked.

In addition, I have the scars the acne left behind to look at every day in the mirror.

So how did I cope? Well, to compensate for the acne and try to cover it up, I began wearing a lot of makeup.

One day I felt challenged by God to go out to eat with my husband, CJ, without wearing one drop of makeup.

Go out in public without any makeup? Surely not.

So I asked God, "Are you sure you want me to do this?"

You see, I was using makeup as a means of self-protection and to feel better about myself. So to go out without any makeup literally felt like I was leaving the house naked! How embarrassing and devastating.

After some resistance, I finally obeyed God that night and left without a trace of makeup. After a few minutes, I couldn't stand it any longer, so I asked my husband if he noticed anything different about my appearance.

He looked at me and hesitantly said, "You're wearing a new headband?"

I said, "Yes, I am wearing a new headband, but do you notice anything else about my appearance?"

He said, "No, I don't."

When I told him I was not wearing any makeup, he responded, "I think you look more beautiful without all the caked-on makeup anyway."

How ironic.

I felt exposed, naked, and self-conscious, but he did not even notice. In fact, he affirmed my natural beauty.

What I learned from that experiment is most people do not notice my imperfections nearly as much as I do. I am so much harder on myself than anyone else could ever be.

What Is the Truth?

The truth is that my value comes from God, my Creator, and not from my appearance and what others think of me.

God is teaching me this truth. He is teaching me that my value comes from Him and not from my outward appearance. It is okay to desire beauty—that is a God-given desire—but I am learning not to base my value on it.

Over the years, I have talked with many teen girls and women who struggle with an eating disorder—bulimia, anorexia, or binge eating. What I found is that body image issues tend to be connected with eating disorders.

Although I have not personally struggled with an eating disorder, my desire to look a certain way has impacted me deeply. Finding my true beauty in Christ and not in my outward appearance has set me free from perfectionism, a shopping addiction, and low self-worth.

Once God began to heal my heart in this area of body image, an inner beauty began to shine out through my eyes, my smile, and my personality. Now, most people tell me they don't even notice my acne scars.

Even Marilyn Monroe said, "A smile is the best makeup a girl could wear,"[2] and I agree.

I still see all my imperfections. We are our own worst critics. Others often see us much differently than we see ourselves.

However, if we will allow Him, God will take our imperfections—our broken crayons—and create something beautiful, a masterpiece.

It's Time to Color!

As you begin to consider your own brokenness, seek to hear from God. Ask Him for His Spirit to wash over you as you color.

Download printable coloring pages from this book here: www.brokencrayonsbook.com

Reflection Questions:

While you color, I encourage you to reflect, pray, and meditate on these questions:

1. What has been my biggest struggle related to body image?

2. Have I tried to compensate for the flaws I see in myself? If so, how?

3. Do I believe this truth today: "my value comes from God, my Creator, and not from my appearance and what others think of me"? What is holding me back from fully embracing who I am in Christ?

4. Optional: stand in front of a mirror and repeat the phrase "I am fearfully and wonderfully made" several times (or choose one of the affirmations based on Scripture listed below). Consider writing this phrase on your bathroom mirror as a reminder each day.

    I am accepted (Ephesians 1:6)

    I am cherished (Ephesians 5:29)

    I am chosen (1 Peter 2:9)

    I am complete in Christ (Colossians 2:10)

    I am created in His image (Genesis 1:27)

    I am forgiven (1 John 1:9)

    I am cared for (1 Peter 5:7)

    I am precious (Isaiah 43:4)

    I am a new creation (2 Corinthians 5:17)

    I am pleasing to God (Psalm 149:4)

    I am protected (Psalm 91:14)

I am set free (John 8:32)

I live in victory (1 Corinthians 15:57)

I am treasured (Psalm 83:3)

I am valuable (Luke 12:24)

Prayer

Lord, I thank you that I am fearfully and wonderfully made. Even though the world shouts that I am not enough and that I never measure up, I choose to find my value in you. Thank you for your patience with me and walking with me step-by-step through this journey. I love you. In Jesus' name I pray, amen.

Hide His Word in Your Heart

This week's memory verse is Psalm 139:14:

I praise you because I am fearfully and wonderfully made;
your works are wonderful,
I know that full well.

Going Deeper

Watch the video for Chapter Three here:
www.brokencrayonsbook.com/video-three

Chapter Three
Viewer's Guide

I praise you because I am fearfully and wonderfully made; your works
are wonderful, I know that full well.

—Psalm 139:14

Every period of history has held its _____ on what was and
was not considered beautiful.

What do we learn from history? That the standard of beauty
_____.

"Jesus Christ is the _____ yesterday and today and forever"
(Heb. 13:8).

One of the biggest influences on us today is the media. And
unfortunately the media is _____ to you.

"For what shall it profit a man, if he shall gain the whole world, and
_____?" (Mark 8:36 KJV).

"Do you not know that your bodies are temples of the Holy Spirit, who is in
you, whom you have received from God? You are not your own; you were
bought at a price. Therefore _____ with your bodies" (1 Cor.
6:19–20).

"The thief comes only to steal and kill and _____; I have come that they may have life, and have it to the full" (John 10:10).

In the original Greek, the definition for the word "destroy" is

_____.[3]

"Then you will know the truth, and the truth will set you

_____" (John 8:32).

God says, "I completely, thoroughly, and perfectly love you, _____, and approve of you. You are mine. I have chosen you."

Your Next Steps

1. Memorize this week's theme verse.
2. Use the reflection questions in Chapter Three.
3. Read Chapter Four.

The "Who Am I?" poem shared in this presentation can be found in the Appendix.

Chapter Four:

~~Hidden and Rejected~~ It's Time to SHINE

I think deep down we all have the desire to belong and be accepted.

I played flute in high school and was actually pretty talented; I believe I had a gift.

Why?

Well, for one reason, music is in my blood. My dad took college courses to be a professional trombonist before he became a pastor, and he still plays the trombone today. My mom has been a music teacher, a music therapist, and a music pastor as well.

On top of that, I was chosen to be first chair in the flute section of band my freshman year.

At my school, being in the band was not popular. Kids would actually call us names and make fun of us. One of the names they called us was a derogatory term: "Band Fags."

Basically, I was bullied because I had the gift of music.

I had a gift that I believe God gave me; however, I felt so much pressure and desperately wanted to fit in with my peers that I ended up quitting band after my freshman year. To this day it brings tears to my eyes thinking about the missed opportunities and all I gave up simply because I wanted to belong.

I had so much God-given potential, but I allowed the rejection of others to impact the course of my life.

I hid.

I shrunk back.

It reminds me of the parable of the talents in Matthew 25:14–30. The person who had been given one talent said, "I was afraid and went out and hid your gold in the ground" (Matt. 25:25).

I think so many times the same thing happens with us: we are afraid and so we hide.

We might be afraid of rejection. We might fear becoming an outcast. We might fear failure.

I believe each one of us has been given gifts from God.

My theme verse for my business is Matthew 5:14–16, which says,

> *"You are the light of the world. A town built on a hill cannot be hidden. Neither do people light a lamp and put it under a bowl. Instead they put it on its stand, and it gives light to everyone in the house. In the same way, let your light shine before others, that they may see your good deeds and glorify your Father in heaven."*

Why must we let our light shine?

- So that everyone will like us?
- So that everyone will tell us how amazing we are?
- So that everyone will notice us and give us a pat on the back?

No.

We let our light shine so that everyone will praise our heavenly Father.

It is not about being self-centered or prideful. It is about giving God the glory and the praise He deserves from the gifts He has given us.

Strong's Concordance is an index of every word in the Bible and can give insight into the original meaning of Scripture in Greek and Hebrew.

The Greek word for shine is *lampo*; it is similar to the English word lamp. *Strong's Concordance* refers to it as a primary verb, meaning it is an action word. The definition is "to beam, i.e. radiate brilliancy (literally or figuratively):—give light, shine."[4]

I love it! We are to radiate the brilliancy of Christ through our lives.

We are to let Him take our broken crayons and create a masterpiece.

I find it interesting that the Greek word for deeds in Matthew 5:16 is *ergon*. When I was a physical therapist, I was trained as an expert in ergonomics. Ergon means "to work."[5]

Strong's definition for ergon is to "toil (as an effort or occupation); by implication, an act:—deed, doing, labour, work."[6]

Our good deeds are the things we do. This includes our work, anything accomplished by our hands, our acts, deeds, or pretty much anything we produce.

- This includes our careers.
- It includes our hobbies, like singing in the choir, painting, or writing.
- It includes other gifts as well, like the gift of hospitality or encouraging others.

Our ultimate goal as followers of Christ is to allow our "good deeds" to glorify God. We are to live out Matthew 5:14–16 every day.

I just got chills.

I don't know about you, but this gets me excited. It is one reason I am so passionate about seeing God bring healing to your broken pieces as He has done with mine.

Deep down, we all long to be accepted.

We want to fit in.

However, we live in a broken, imperfect world and eventually we will face the pain of rejection.

It hurts! It is not easy.

They say hindsight is 20/20. Today, we feel the pain of the rejection. Later, we may be able to see that the rejection was a redirection or even a protection from something we could not see at the time.

Not long ago I tried out for the worship team at our church. I had the worst tryout of my life. It was horrible and embarrassing.

As a result, I was excluded from being part of the ministry. I felt rejected. It was painful because I know I can sing much better than I did that day.

However, now I can reframe the rejection as a redirection. Weeks after I was rejected by the worship team, God opened an opportunity for CJ and me to receive training for the counseling ministry at our church. This would not have happened if I had accepted a position on the worship team.

I don't understand all the reasons for rejection. People say hurtful things. We make mistakes. Doors are slammed shut in our faces.

Sometimes the brokenness that results from the criticism or rejection of others causes us to hide. Sometimes our own stinkin' thinkin' stops us from shining bright.

Some days we feel we are not enough. Other days we feel like we are too much.

And there are days we simply want to hide under the covers and never come out. I actually had several of those days recently while writing this book.

However, I want to encourage each one of you today to be willing to give your gifts to God anew. Find your acceptance in the One who created you. You are loved.

- You are not defined by the opinions of others.
- You are not defined by your past mistakes.
- You are not defined by your successes or failures.

In Christ:

- You are enough.
- You are valuable and loved.
- You are fearfully and wonderfully made.

Joshua 1:9 says, "Have I not commanded you? Be strong and courageous. Do not be afraid; do not be discouraged, for the Lord your God will be with you wherever you go."

Be willing to step out of the shadows. Even if you still feel rejected. Even if you have made many mistakes. Even if you still doubt God's love.

You have been hiding long enough.

It is time to let your light shine!

It's Time to Color!

As you begin to consider your own brokenness, seek to hear from God. Ask Him for His Spirit to wash over you as you color.

Download printable coloring pages from this book here:
www.brokencrayonsbook.com

Reflection Questions:

While you color, I encourage you to reflect, pray, and meditate on these questions:

1. What gifts has God given me?
2. How have I hidden those gifts due to fear of rejection or failure?
3. In what ways have I faced rejection (big or small)?
4. What is one thing I can do to come out of the shadows and let the light of Christ shine through me today?

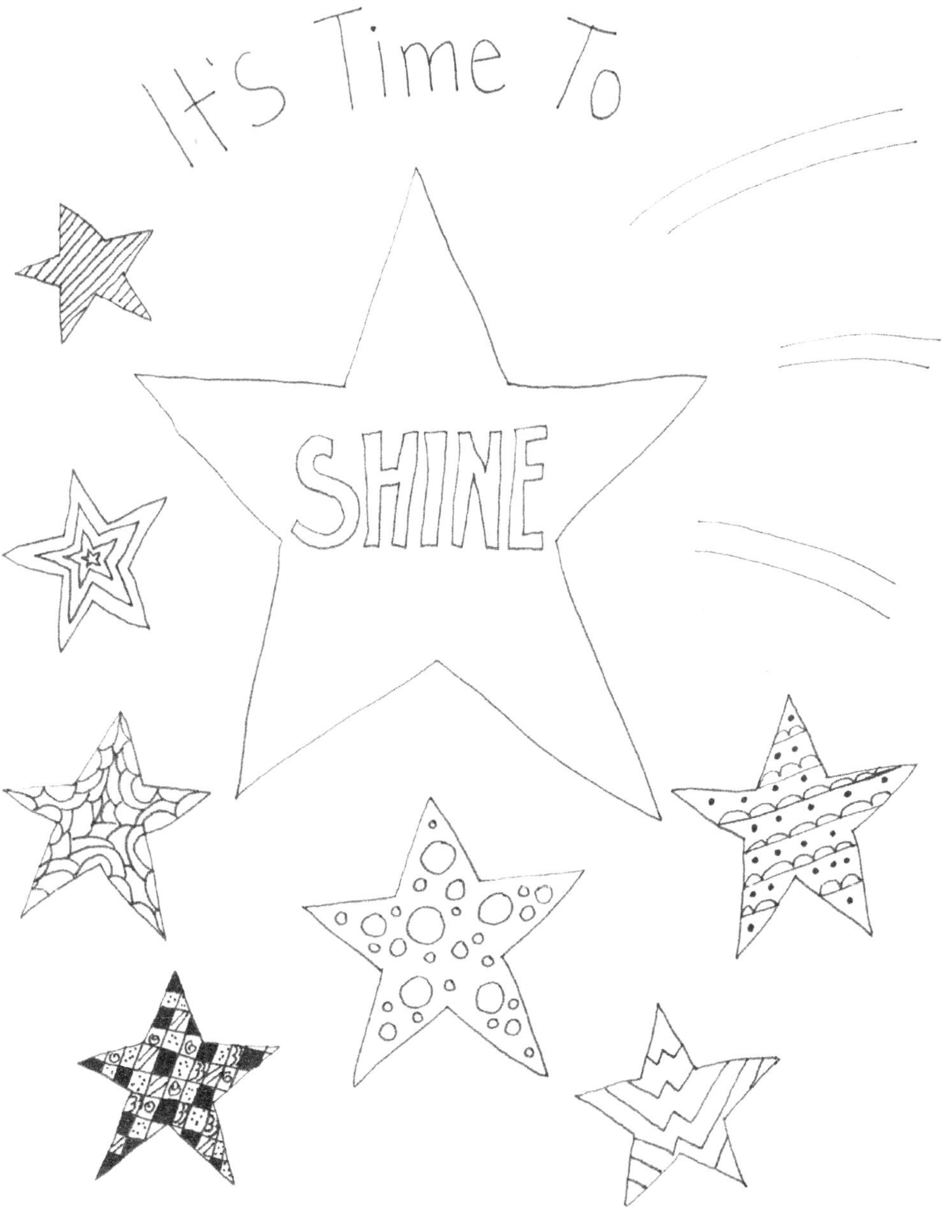
It's Time To
SHINE

Prayer

Lord, I thank you for new starts and second chances. I thank you for your grace. I pray you would help me to discover and embrace all the gifts you have given me. Help me to heal from any rejection in the past and to know that I am fully loved and accepted in you. Give me the courage I need to come out of the shadows and to let your light shine brightly through me today. In Jesus' name I pray, amen.

Hide His Word in Your Heart

This week's memory verse is Matthew 5:16:

> *In the same way, let your light shine before others, that they may see your good deeds and glorify your Father in heaven.*

Going Deeper

Watch the video for Chapter Four here:
www.brokencrayonsbook.com/video-four

Chapter Four
Viewer's Guide

In the same way, let your light shine before others, that they may see your good deeds and glorify your Father in heaven.

—Matthew 5:16

"You belong to your father, the devil, and you want to carry out your father's desires. He was a murderer from the beginning, not holding to the truth, for there is no truth in him. When he lies, he speaks his native language, for he is a _____ and the father of _____" (John 8:44).

Weed Recognition: 3 Types of Thoughts

1. _____ thoughts: *analytical, problem-solving, connected* *(1+1=2)*

2. _____ thoughts: *accusing, lying, condemning*

3. _____ thoughts: *comforting, teaching, helping*

How Do You Cope with Rejection?

☐ Perfectionism

☐ People pleasing

☐ Striving

☐ Hiding

☐ Other: _____

If you need other examples, see this online resource: http://negativeemotionslist.com

5 Steps to Replace the Lies with the Truth

1. Recognize the lies (i.e., weed recognition). (John 10:10)
2. Take our stand in the spiritual battle. Command Satan and his demons to leave in the authority of Jesus' name. When we resist the devil, he will flee from us. (Ephesians 6:10–18, James 4:7)
3. Uproot the lie by confessing our sin of believing the lie (and any other sin we acted on because of the lie). (1 John 1:9)
4. Repent, asking for God's forgiveness for living our lives based upon the lies. (Luke 5:32)
5. Replace the lies with God's truth. Invite Jesus to come and the Holy Spirit to fill us with His truth (the opposite of the lie). (John 8:32)

Your Next Steps

1. Memorize this week's theme verse.
2. Use the reflection questions in Chapter Four.
3. Read Chapter Five.

The books referenced in this video, examples of replacing lies with truth, and the Belief Filter image can be found in the Appendix.

Chapter Five:

~~Devastated by Tragedy~~ Faith in a Sovereign God

It was June 2009 and I had no clue how drastically my life would soon change. I thought some of my worst days were over. I thought that I had dealt with enough major trials for one lifetime.

However, on July 1, 2009, that all changed when my dad, Chuck Sandstrom, was assaulted. Once again, a violent act was committed against our family. Dealing with my grandma's murder was one of the most difficult things I ever dealt with, but this time it hit even closer to home, my dad.

Dad was assaulted so severely that it left him in a coma for almost six weeks and resulted in a severe Traumatic Brain Injury (TBI).

At first I was in shock, completely numb.

But eventually, many emotions began to surface: anger, grief, pain, bitterness.

I heard myself saying, "Lord, it's not fair. Why our family, AGAIN? I don't know if I can handle this."

I realized it was time for me to walk through the path of forgiveness once again and choose to trust God with the pain, the hurt, and the unknowns of this tragedy. And He led me down a path to find hope—hope in the midst of tragedy.

I won't lie to you. It has not been an easy road. But looking back, I can see God's presence with us every step of the way. Every tear, every emotion, every joy, every disappointment. He has been here.

I have found out once again that what Jesus teaches is applicable to real life. In the midst of pain, tragedy, and some of the most difficult days of my life, Jesus brought me hope.

And He wants to do the same for you, if you will seek Him and apply His teachings to your life.

I recently heard the word hope described with this acronym: Hold On, Pain Ends. And I have found that to be so true in my own life.

Punched in the Stomach

While my dad was in recovery, I decided to go to a conference all about Traumatic Brain Injuries (TBIs).

There was one point in the conference, after hearing many stories and being taught all the functions of the brain, when I felt as if I had been punched in the stomach. I began to feel like I was going to get sick and vomit. Literally.

Thankfully, the instructor decided to take an early lunch.

The Emotions Tumbled Out

I could barely make it to my truck before the sobs escaped. I started driving to lunch and then decided to just pull off in an isolated part of the parking lot.

I cried and cried.

I felt so angry that this happened to my dad. I started screaming, "It's unfair!" over and over while beating the truck seat.

I was grieving the losses my dad might face and those our family might face. The thought even went through my mind that I would rather have him pass away peacefully than have him live with any residual deficits. And then I felt guilty for even thinking that.

Up and down my emotions swirled.

And then I decided to turn on my worship music. I found the song by Kim Hill "You Are Still Holy" and sat crying as I listened to it.

My Chevy Colorado Became a Sanctuary

I allowed myself to feel my emotions, cry, and let them pass through. As the song "You Alone" by Kim Hill started playing, God brought back to my mind a story my mom had reminded me of the day before.

It's a story Corrie ten Boom shares. She says that whenever her family traveled anywhere on the train when she was a little girl, her dad would keep their tickets. And then, at just the right time, as they boarded the train, he would hand Corrie her ticket.

In the same way, I sensed God saying to me that He has my "ticket" right now. My "ticket" represents Dad's prognosis, outcome, and the answers to all of my questions. And when I need these answers, He will give them to me at just the right time. Until then, I can trust Him with all the unknowns, the unanswered questions, and the pain. I am in a waiting phase even now.

Missing My Dad

I have waves of missing my dad. He is still physically present with us, but he has changed so much as a result of his TBI. One day as I sat in my car, I didn't hear an audible voice, but I sensed God saying to me as I was journaling:

> Shelley, I love you. I am your heavenly Father. And I love you. I know that your earthly father isn't able to show his love for you right now, but I am able to. If you'll let me. It's hard because of the anger, hurt, and other emotions. But realize I am not the author of pain or hurt or violence. What I created in the garden of Eden was devoid of that. Heaven will be devoid of that. I know it's hard to understand and I don't expect you to. The big question you have is "Why do I allow it?"

> Think of your two-year-old niece, Allie, trying to understand calculus and physics. No matter how much she tries, it just won't make sense to her yet. And the same is true for you. You can wrack your brain and think and analyze and study and discuss and still never figure it all out yet . . . on this side of heaven. Right now, what it boils down to is your view of me and your trust in me.

I admit that I don't have all the answers. I'm convinced there are certain things I won't completely understand this side of heaven. But as I sat in my truck, a peace began to return to me.

Finding Safety in the Storm

In the midst of this tragedy, I have sensed God saying to me that He is here with me and that I can find safety and refuge in Him, even when I feel like everything around me is uncertain and feels unsafe. "The Lord is my rock, my fortress and my deliverer; my God is my rock, in whom I take refuge, my shield and the horn of my salvation, my stronghold" (Ps. 18:2).

I got a picture of what that safe "refuge" looks like for me.

There may be times when I have to go out in the storm and get wet and cold. But I know that God is always with me. He will never leave me or forsake me. And whenever I need rest, my safe place is waiting for me.

I pictured that safe refuge as a warm inviting cave where I am protected from the storms. God offers me warmth by the fire to dry off and food for my soul. He says, "Come to Me, all who are weary and heavy-laden, and I will give you rest" (Matt. 11:28 NASB).

He walks with me. He doesn't stay behind in the cave. He will be with me to give me the strength and wisdom I need to navigate this storm.

Storms come and go, and I can't predict when they will come.

This is a storm that has entered my life. I was not expecting or planning my dad to be assaulted, resulting in a coma and a severe brain injury. But now I have to deal with it—kind of like floods, wildfires, hurricanes, and earthquakes are unexpected disasters that leave behind so much damage.

I feel like my life is in rubble again. It feels as if my heart is broken and hurting.

Rebuilding After a "Storm"

As I journaled one day while my dad was still in a coma, this is what I sensed God saying to me:

Shelley, you may feel like your life is in rubble again, but realize that I am able to "restore what the locusts have eaten" and I am the Ultimate Rebuilder of hearts and lives. As we work together at "rebuilding the walls" of your life, there will be a greater and deeper beauty seen in you than was evident before. I am able to bring good out of any situation. I am about healing and restoring the brokenhearted.

Beloved, your heart has been broken, but as we rebuild and restore the brokenness within you, there will be a beauty that far exceeds anything you could have imagined before. Trust me. Hold on to my hand as we walk through this storm together. Come take shelter with me and find refuge in me. And surrender your broken heart to me. I am the Healer and Restorer of broken hearts.

And so that day I found peace again in His safe refuge. I was given the hope of a promise. The promise of rebuilding after the storm, the rebuilding of my broken heart.

He heals the brokenhearted and binds up their wounds. (Ps. 147:3)

A Different Type of Grief

To outsiders, it may seem as if today "all is well" and that we're "doing great" now that Dad is out of the coma and able to live on his own again. He is walking, talking, driving, and even working a small part-time job.

However, there is a different type of grief I feel.

There are losses that I face each day as we learn to deal with the long-term effects of Dad's brain injury. It is hard to put into words, but I felt this grief wash over me again when I started reading Lee and Bob Woodruff's book *In an Instant: A Family's Journey of Love and Healing,* which tells the story of Bob's brain injury and his recovery. At this point, my dad was out of the coma and in rehab, but as I read the Woodruffs' description of the early days and the trauma of it all, I felt a fresh grief fall on me.

Things will never be the same.

However, I can trust that every experience God puts in my life has a purpose. He does not waste anything.

Corrie ten Boom, a Nazi prison camp survivor and one of my heroes of the faith, says, "Every experience God gives us, every person He puts in our lives is the perfect preparation for the future that only He can see."[7]

The Moral of the Story?

Until I reach heaven, the storms will continue to come. Pain. Devastation. Heartache. Grief.

Broken crayons.

However, I have the promise that God will walk with me through every single storm.

He will never fail me, He will never leave me or forsake me, and when my life is built upon His foundation, I will survive whatever comes my way.

And you can too. If your foundation is built upon Jesus Christ, it will last no matter what tragedy comes into your life.

We can trust in a sovereign God even when all we see is broken pieces.

Tragedy usually draws us closer to God or further away. I encourage you to bring your broken crayons to God and allow Him to walk with you through whatever you are facing today.

It's Time to Color!

As you begin to consider your own brokenness, seek to hear from God. Ask Him for His Spirit to wash over you as you color.

Download printable coloring pages from this book here: www.brokencrayonsbook.com

Reflection Questions:

While you color, I encourage you to reflect, pray, and meditate on these questions:

1. Has my family been through something tragic that changed my life?

   Your experience might be completely different from ours, but any tragedy can be life altering. Real life isn't always as simple as black and white. The process of recovery isn't all fun and games.

Life is hard. No matter where we are in our road to recovery, it's important to remember that God works all things together for the good of those who love Him (Rom. 8:28), and even when we walk through the valley of the shadow of death, He is with us (Ps. 23:4).

I encourage you to say a prayer asking God to get you through this. Ask Him for the strength that you, and those around you, need to get through this trial, and for Him to continually remind you that He is with you and that things are getting better. Be still and know that He is God.

2. What do I tend to rely on during times of crisis? Do I try to survive on my own strength, or do I trust God to get me through?

    When you start to get weighed down, I encourage you to remember the words Paul wrote in 2 Corinthians 12:9-10: "But he said to me, 'My grace is sufficient for you, for my power is made perfect in weakness.' Therefore I will boast all the more gladly about my weaknesses, so that Christ's power may rest on me. That is why, for Christ's sake, I delight in weaknesses, in insults, in hardships, in persecutions, in difficulties. For when I am weak, then I am strong." Then pray for God to give you His strength.

3. Emotions are God's gift to us. The author of Ecclesiastes wrote that "there is a time for everything, and a season for every activity under the heavens" (3:1). The point is that while it might not be any fun to experience conflicting emotions, it is okay to cry, to hurt, and to grieve. What it's not okay to do is let those emotions control you.

    Right now I encourage you to take the time to grieve but also to cry out to God and put the situation and your emotions in His hands. Ask God to help you through this time and to help you see even small improvements as encouraging

4. Consider setting some time aside to worship God. While the things we are going through are far from easy, it's important to remember that He is still holy.

5. I encourage you to say a prayer and/or turn on some worship music and spend some time worshiping our Creator, then agree to wait upon His timing and trust Him with this tragedy.

6. What do I feel like God is telling me today?

   I encourage you to look for something He might be trying to teach you during this time of healing.

Prayer

Lord, I thank you that I have the promise that you will walk with me through every single storm I face. You will never fail me, you will never leave me or forsake me, and when my life is built upon your foundation, I will survive whatever comes my way. Today, I choose to trust in you, even amidst the broken pieces in my life that I don't understand this side of heaven. I bring my broken crayons to you today. I know I can find peace in the midst of my storm in you. In Jesus' name I pray, amen.

Hide His Word in Your Heart

This week's memory verse is Isaiah 55:8–9:

> *"For my thoughts are not your thoughts,*
> *neither are your ways my ways,"*
> *declares the Lord.*
> *"As the heavens are higher than the earth,*
> *so are my ways higher than your ways*
> *and my thoughts than your thoughts."*

Going Deeper

Watch the video for Chapter Five here:
www.brokencrayonsbook.com/video-five

Chapter Five
Viewer's Guide

"For my thoughts are not your thoughts, neither are your ways
my ways," declares the Lord. "As the heavens are higher than
the earth, so are my ways higher than your ways and
my thoughts than your thoughts."
—Isaiah 55:8–9

Our _____ has the potential to deeply impact our lives
and the decisions we make every day.

How Do You View God?

To you, is God's voice:

- ☐ harsh or loving?
- ☐ condemning or grace-based?
- ☐ angry or caring?
- ☐ critical or accepting?
- ☐ demeaning or affirming?
- ☐ hurtful or kind?
- ☐ far off or close by?
- ☐ silent or present?
- ☐ demanding or fair?
- ☐ perfectionistic or forgiving?

John 16:33, Matthew 5:44–45, James 1:2–4, 12

Three Pictures

1.

2.

3.

It comes down to trust. (Isaiah 55:8–9, 1 Corinthians 13:12)

According to Scripture

- God is changeless. (Malachi 3:6)
- God is all-powerful. (Jeremiah 32:17)
- God is all-knowing. (Romans 11:33–34)
- God is everywhere. (Psalm 139:7–10)
- God is eternal. (Revelation 1:8)
- God is holy. (Exodus 15:11)
- God is love. (Ephesians 3:17–18)
- God is truth. (Numbers 23:19)
- God is wisdom. (Romans 11:33)
- God is just. (Jeremiah 17:10)
- God is compassionate. (James 5:11)
- God is faithful. (Psalm 89:8)

The power of _____.

Your Next Steps

1. Memorize this week's theme verse.
2. Use the reflection questions in Chapter Five.
3. Read Chapter Six.

Chapter Six:

A ~~Broken Cup~~ My Cup Overflows

Growing up, I was insecure. To outsiders, I looked confident, like I had it "all together." But on the inside, I was broken and dying a little more each day.

I was really good at hiding my brokenness. You see, no one knew the real Shelley because I was ashamed of my true self. I thought that if people knew who I really was on the inside, they would reject me.

As a result, I felt a deep ache and an emptiness that nothing seemed to fill. No matter what I did, the ache would not go away. I tried to fill this void with many things, including the attention of guys. However, when a guy rejected me, the emptiness would return.

I also tried to perfect my looks. Some days I would feel on top of the world because I had a "good hair day." However, if I had a "bad hair day" or received a negative comment about my looks, I would plummet into insecurity again. I rode this roller coaster of emotions up and down and never found true satisfaction.

The Broken Cup Illustration

Eventually, God gave me an illustration of a broken cup. Several tragedies in my life—including my grandma's murder, an instance of sexual abuse, the loss of two cousins in separate car accidents, my parents' divorce, and the list goes on—represented cracks in my cup and the brokenness that came into my life. However, instead of bringing my broken cup, my pain and brokenness, to God for healing, I was trying to deal with it myself.

And so the illustration is this: I was trying to fill my broken cup with water from several sources (i.e., seeking guys' attention, perfecting my looks, etc.) to fill the emptiness I felt inside. But no matter what I did, it did not satisfy because my "cup" was equipped to hold only one kind of water, the living water of Jesus. The kind of water I tried to fill it with would simply drain out over time. So although I would feel temporary satisfaction, it never lasted.

Why?

Well, as Oswald Chambers says, "No love of the natural heart is safe unless the human heart has been satisfied by God first."[8]

Wanting to look good is not necessarily wrong in and of itself. However, I learned that trying to satisfy my heart with anything other than God became an idol in my life, and therefore I never felt satisfied. The other fixes were only temporary.

Jeremiah 2:13 says,

> *"My people have committed two sins:*
> *They have forsaken me,*
>   *the spring of living water,*
> *and have dug their own cisterns,*
>   *broken cisterns that cannot hold water."*

I sensed God saying to me, "Shelley, you have committed two sins: you have forsaken me, the spring of living water, and no matter what you do, you will never be satisfied apart from me. I want you to come to my spring of living water that never runs dry."

I am sure some of you have felt the same way.

A Cup That Overflows

I walked through a season in my life when God asked me to surrender my brokenness, my broken cup, to Him for healing. It was a painful season as I began to face some deep wounds from my past. However, over time, as I surrendered my broken cup to God, He put all my broken pieces inside His cup, His cup that no longer had any cracks and was able to hold water. As I chose to come to Him each day for His living water, my emptiness was replaced with true satisfaction in Christ.

If you put a mug underneath a waterfall, what will happen?

The cup will fill with water and then eventually overflow.

And that is what began to happen in my heart. As I was filled with Christ each day, I was not only satisfied in Christ but His Spirit in me began to overflow.

Instead of being needy and going to other people to feel good about myself, I actually had something to give to others. I had love to give. I had joy to give. I had encouragement to share.

Psalm 23:5 says, "My cup overflows."

I love how the Amplified Version, Classic Edition (AMPC) says it: "My [brimming] cup runs over." This is a wonderful picture of having more than enough.

Philippians 4:19 (AMP) says, "And my God will liberally supply (fill until full) your every need according to His riches in glory in Christ Jesus."

Do we truly believe that God is going to fill us to the full?

More often than I care to admit, I find myself simply scraping by, barely getting through the day. Have you ever felt that way? I still have days where I pray, "Lord, help me just get through this day." I start thinking like a minimalist again.

However, God is asking me to change my thinking and instead pray, "Lord, fill me to the full! How do you want to use me today?"

The Chrysalis

"Therefore, if anyone is in Christ, the new creation has come: The old has gone, the new is here!" (2 Cor. 5:17).

I love the story of the chrysalis: a caterpillar that spends time in a cocoon and finally emerges as a beautiful butterfly. It takes time for the caterpillar to become a butterfly. In fact, if someone would try to speed up the process and cut open the cocoon early, the butterfly would die. It has to go through the entire process in order to emerge as something completely different, a masterpiece.

Most of the time in our culture, we look for an instant fix. We look for instant gratification instead of allowing God to take us through the entire process of healing He has for us.

Some of us may still be caterpillars; we may still be seeking and searching spiritually.

Some of us may be in the cocoon where God is doing a major work of healing in our lives.

And then some of us may have emerged from the cocoon as changed, a beautiful butterfly that God is using in powerful ways.

John 10:10 says, "The thief comes only to steal and kill and destroy; I [Jesus] have come that [you] may have life, and have it to the full."

The enemy plans to destroy you. But Jesus has come so that you can have life—and have it to the full.

It's Time to Color!

As you begin to consider your own brokenness, seek to hear from God. Ask Him for His Spirit to wash over you as you color.

Download printable coloring pages from this book here: www.brokencrayonsbook.com

Reflection Questions:

While you color, I encourage you to reflect, pray, and meditate on these questions:

1. Do I relate at all to Shelley's broken cup story? If so, how?
2. In what ways have I tried to satisfy myself apart from God?
3. Am I willing and ready to start a lifelong journey of finding my satisfaction in Christ alone?
4. What, if anything, is standing in my way? What will I now do to overcome the obstacles I have identified?

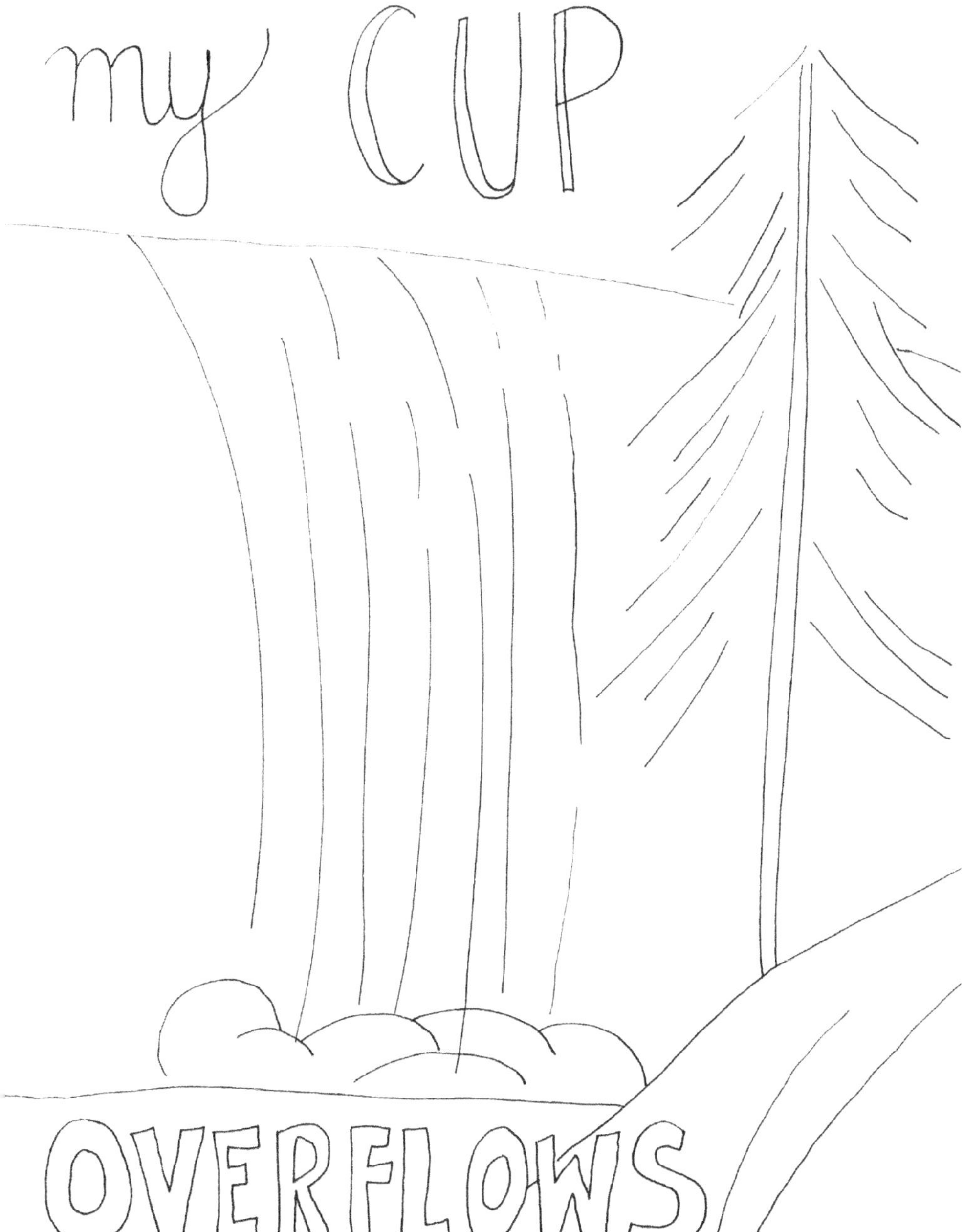
my CUP
OVERFLOWS

Prayer

Lord, thank you for providing a way to bring healing to my broken pieces. Thank you for Jesus' death on the cross for my sins and for the Holy Spirit who helps me each day. Help me to bring my brokenness and emptiness to you each day. Thank you for filling me with your love and your joy and for giving me a renewed purpose in my life. I love you. In Jesus' name I pray, amen.

Hide His Word in Your Heart

This week's memory verse is Psalm 23:5:

> *You prepare a table before me*
> *   in the presence of my enemies.*
> *You anoint my head with oil;*
> *   my cup overflows.*

Going Deeper

Watch the video for Chapter Six here:
www.brokencrayonsbook.com/video-six

Chapter Six
Viewer's Guide

You prepare a table before me in the presence of my enemies. You anoint my head with oil; my cup overflows.

—Psalm 23:5

"My people have committed two sins: They have _____, the spring of living water, and have dug their own cisterns, _____ that cannot hold water" (Jer. 2:13).

My Broken Cup Restored

1.   The first step was _____.

2.   Then, _____.

3.   Finally _____.

"Pain is inevitable, misery is _____." —Hyrum W. Smith[9]

Your Next Steps

1.   Memorize this week's theme verse.
2.   Use the reflection questions in Chapter Six.
3.   Read the Conclusion.

Conclusion

Although this book and video study is now coming to an end, your healing journey has just begun.

When you have a relationship with God, He provides His Holy Spirit to lead and guide you. You are not alone.

I have included a few books for recommended reading in the Appendix, and you can listen to others' stories in our Broken Crayons Still Color podcast here:

www.brokencrayonsbook.com/podcast

I pray that you continue to seek God in your life every day. He is able to take your broken crayons and create a masterpiece!

God's Promise

It was Independence Day weekend 2002. I stayed in a small cabin in the woods called "The Hermitage" for a silent retreat. It was a time to meet with God, hear from Him, and receive His healing.

It was during that weekend I finally forgave my grandma's murderer.

In my journal I wrote, "Lord, today I am starting over new, a new creation. I broke free from the cocoon and now am ready to fly as a butterfly."

I knew that weekend was a turning point in my life.

I wrote what I sensed God saying to me during a time of prayer in my journal: "Shelley, there is redemption in the midst of this particular sorrow because I will use this story and your process of healing to impact eternity for many, many people. Through this difficult experience, you will be able to comfort others with the comfort you have received."

He then led me to read Isaiah 61:1–3:

> *The Spirit of the Sovereign Lord is on me,*
>   *because the Lord has anointed me*
>   *to proclaim good news to the poor.*
> *He has sent me to bind up the brokenhearted,*
>   *to proclaim freedom for the captives*
>   *and release from darkness for the prisoners,*
> *to proclaim the year of the Lord's favor*
>   *and the day of vengeance of our God,*
> *to comfort all who mourn,*
>   *and provide for those who grieve in Zion—*
> *to bestow on them a crown of beauty*
>   *instead of ashes,*
> *the oil of joy*
>   *instead of mourning,*
> *and a garment of praise*
>   *instead of a spirit of despair.*
> *They will be called oaks of righteousness,*
>   *a planting of the Lord*
>   *for the display of his splendor.*

Isaiah 61:1 is now my life verse because of how God has taken the broken pieces of my heart and brought freedom and healing. And I believe this book is simply one way God is using the healing He has brought in my life to impact many for eternity.

So many times I wanted to quit while writing this book and recording the video series. It has honestly been very difficult for me to revisit the pain from the past and share in such a vulnerable way.

My prayer is that this book gave you hope and started you on your own path to freedom and healing.

All for Him,

Shelley Hitz

Appendix

Recommended Resources

Books

Biblical Healing and Deliverance: A Guide to Experiencing Freedom from Sins of the Past, Destructive Beliefs, Emotional and Spiritual Pain, Curses and Oppression by Chester and Betsy Kylstra (Chosen Books, 2005)

Waking the Dead: The Glory of a Heart Fully Alive by John Eldredge (Thomas Nelson, 2005)

Breaking Free: Discover the Victory of Total Surrender by Beth Moore (B&H Books, 2007)

You Are What You Believe: Simple Steps to Transform Your Life by Hyrum W. Smith (Berrett-Koehler Publishers, 2016)

Healing the Wounded Heart: Removing Obstacles to Intimacy with God by Thom Gardner (Destiny Image Publishers, 2005)

The Healing Journey: An Interactive Guide to Spiritual Wholeness by Thom Gardner (Destiny Image Publishers, 2010)

A Christian Woman's Guide to Breaking Free from Pornography: It's Not Just a Guy's Problem by Shelley Hitz (Body and Soul Publishing, 2012)

A Life of Gratitude: 21 Days to Overcoming Self-Pity and Negativity by Shelley Hitz (Body and Soul Publishing, 2012)

Forgiveness Formula: Finding Lasting Freedom in Christ by CJ and Shelley Hitz (Body and Soul Publishing, 2011)

Other Resources

Freedom Groups:

I recommend watching the introduction video from the Freedom Groups series. It is currently available to watch online here:

www.shelleyhitz.com/freedomgroups

Steps to Freedom:

I recommend you take this step even further by going through Neil Anderson's "Steps to Freedom in Christ." Our ministry has been given permission to use this valuable resource with those we counsel and minister to. Contact us here to get more information and download this powerful guide here:

www.shelleyhitz.com/freedom

Warrior's Prayer:

It is important to realize that we are in a spiritual battle. And to prepare, the Bible tells us in Ephesians 6 that we are to put on our spiritual armor. I recommend praying through Ephesians 6:10–20 and asking God to protect you with His armor each morning before you begin your day. You can read the warrior's prayer based on these Scriptures here:

www.shelleyhitz.com/warrior

Clinging Cross:

When my dad was in the hospital in a coma, I found a Clinging Cross in the gift shop. There were many days I didn't know how to pray or what to pray and would simply hold the cross that fit perfectly into the shape of my hand and ask God for help.

Sometimes having something tangible to represent God's presence in our lives can be helpful when walking through difficult times. It makes a nice gift for others as well. You can find this resource here:

www.shelleyhitz.com/clingingcross

Share Your Story in a Book

Have you dreamed about writing and publishing a book? A book is a powerful way to share your testimony!

If God is calling you to write a book, Shelley coaches authors on the process of writing, self-publishing, and marketing books in her online academy here:

www.authoraudienceacademy.com

Broken Crayons Still Color Podcast

Listen to others' stories in our Broken Crayons Still Color podcast here: www.brokencrayonsbook.com/podcast

You can also apply to be featured on our podcast and share your story here: www.shelleyhitz.com/story

"Who Am I?" Poem

I had what I would call an "identity crisis" years ago. I wrote this poem as I began to find my true identity in Christ. I had an encounter with God during a time of worship at a conference, and afterward God gave me this poem to describe my experience. Maybe you can relate to my struggles to find my true identity.

Who Am I?

My first answer would probably be my name. But my name does not describe who I am on the inside.

I could then give the title of my profession. But that is what I do.

I could then tell you I am a wife, a sister, and a daughter. But those are my relationships.

I ask again . . . Who am I?

I could describe myself as an extrovert and outgoing. That is my personality.

I am organized in planning events. But that is a gift God has given me.

I could describe my appearance, but that is not who I am either.

So many times I have believed what others say I am. If I receive affirmation, then I feel worthwhile.

However, when I receive criticism, then I feel like a failure. I have chosen to ride the roller coaster of emotions instead of believing the truth of what God says about me.

I have tried to work harder to prove that I am worthwhile. Yet every time I mess up or fail, I am reminded that I will never measure up.

I will never be pretty enough or talented enough. I will never be skinny enough or do enough good things for the church. I will never be a good enough wife or sister or daughter.

But I keep trying harder and harder.

I believe the lie that if I continue to try harder, I will finally be "good" enough.

One day, God gently said to me,

"Stop trying so hard to prove yourself to others. Get your worth from me. I've already given it to you. Remember my grace. It's a free gift and nothing you can achieve by trying harder.

Rest in my grace.

You are working so hard to have a certain position in the eyes of others, to be well liked, and to have popularity. You want to be appreciated for what you do.

But I want you to know that you already have an elevated position.

Because you have a relationship with my Son, Jesus Christ, you are a part of my Kingdom as my daughter and coheir with Christ. Because you are the daughter of a King, you are given the position of being a princess.

You are my princess, a royal princess.

Remember that an earthly princess is not special because of who she is or what she does; she has status and position because of who her dad is: a king. She has royalty in her blood.

You have royalty in your blood as well.

You are the daughter of a King. And no matter what you do, your status will never change.

I have chosen you and I have a plan for your life.

I will not forget you and I will be with you always.

I have engraved you in the palm of my hands.

Rest in the knowledge of who you are in me.

Nothing else will ever be enough.

You are my daughter and I love you!"

Belief Filter

For a full explanation of the Belief Filter, see the video that corresponds with Chapter Four.

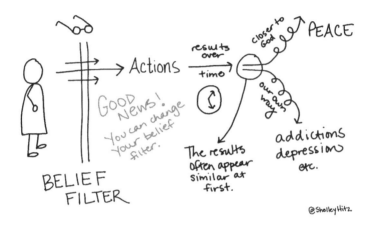

Replacing the Lies with the Truth

Here are seven of the lies I have personally struggled with that you can use as examples of how to replace the enemy's lies with God's Truth.

Lie: I should not have to live with unfulfilled longings.

Truth: I will always have unfulfilled longings this side of heaven. The deepest longings of my heart cannot be filled by any created thing. If I will accept them, unfulfilled longings will increase my longing for God and for heaven. (Romans 8:23–25; Ephesians 3:11; Hebrews 11:13–16; Psalm 16:11, 73:25; Deuteronomy 8:3; Psalm 34:8–10; Philippians 3:20, 4:1)

~~*~*

Lie: God is not really enough.

Truth: God is enough. If I have Him, I have all I need. (Psalm 23:1, 73:23–26; Colossians 2:9–10)

Lie: When I am alone, I am lonely and rejected by others.

Truth: I can enjoy spending time by myself because my Father is always with me— He will never leave me. I am chosen, treasured, and loved by Him. (Matthew 28:20; Deuteronomy 26:18)

~~*~*

Lie: I cannot trust God because He has let me down in the past.

Truth: God is faithful and has my best interests in mind, even when I can't understand His ways. He will help me begin to trust Him again. He wants me to trust Him and I want to trust Him. (Lamentations 3:5–6; Isaiah 55:9; Proverbs 3:5–6; Psalm 91:1–3)

~~*~*

Lie: I am not worthy of love.

Truth: The Father loves me completely, thoroughly, and perfectly. There's nothing I can do to add or detract from that love. (Isaiah 54:10)

~~*~*

Lie: I am afraid of what the future holds.

Truth: God has plans for me—to prosper me and not to harm me, to give me a hope and a future. I can trust Him with my future. He is walking before me, preparing the way. (Jeremiah 29:11; Isaiah 43:18–19)

~~*~*

Lie: I am ashamed of and regret my decisions and mistakes of the past. I can't forgive myself for what I have done.

Truth: I am free from condemnation. I am precious and honored in the eyes of my Father. I value God's opinion of me more than my past or what others think of me. My value comes from being the daughter of the King. (Romans 8:1–2; Isaiah 43:4; Romans 8:15–17)

~~*~*

I encourage you to come up with your own. Search the Scriptures using tools like www.BibleGateway.com, www.YouVersion.com, or www.BlueLetterBible.org to find Scriptures that relate to what you are going through. Reword them into truths that you can carry with you and repeat until they replace the lies you have been believing!

Leader's Guide

This guide will help you as you facilitate this book study with a group. My hope and prayer is that many groups will go through the book together. There is power in community and learning from each other.

As Dr. Larry Crabb explains, "I have come to believe that the root of all our personal and emotional difficulties is a lack of togetherness, a failure to connect that keeps us from receiving life and prevents life in us from spilling over onto others. I therefore believe that the surest route to overcoming problems and becoming the people we were meant to be is reconnecting with God and with our community."[10]

I believe each group will be unique in how you go through this material. I have suggestions for you, but follow the leading of the Holy Spirit. As you get to know your group participants, you'll have a better idea of which questions to ask. Some groups will be ready for deep discussion right away and others will not. Ultimately, I encourage you to allow God to give you discernment and direction.

Overview of the Book Study

This leader's guide provides instructions for leading a seven-session book study. Each week contains reading from the book as well as a video teaching that goes deeper into the material to help each person apply it to his or her own life.

The videos are thirty-five to thirty-eight minutes in length, so group sessions should be at least one hour in length. If you would like to have longer discussion times, I recommend scheduling ninety minutes for each session.

The topics in the book and the videos cover material that may bring up emotions for your participants. Make sure to have resources available to recommend if they need one-on-one counseling or help. Several times throughout the book, I recommend the reader follow up with a counselor, pastor, or trusted mentor.

Be in Prayer!

As I was writing the book and recording these videos, I encountered some of the most difficult spiritual attack I have ever faced. I believe this is because the book addresses core issues that can help the reader find lasting freedom and healing in Christ. I had a prayer team praying for me each week, and I recommend you do the same. Find at least two to three people who will be willing to pray for you and the participants of your study during these seven weeks.

Prayer is powerful and can accomplish what our words and efforts cannot.

Please know that I am praying for you and each person who will go through this study. I pray that God brings hope, freedom, and healing to the broken pieces in your life as well as the lives of your group participants.

Suggested Flow for Each Session

You can facilitate this study in the way that works best for your group. Here is a suggested flow for each session.

Open (5 minutes):

- Open in a short prayer.
- Review the memory verse for that week and have the group say it out loud together.
- I do not recommend putting any of your participants on the spot to say the memory verse out loud, but you could ask how they are incorporating the verse into their daily lives. In the Introduction, I share several options for meditating on the weekly memory verse.

Video (approximately 40 minutes):

- Watch the video for each chapter together. You can stream it online from my website or download the video files if you do not have a reliable Internet connection.
- Make sure each participant has a book with the viewer's guide to fill in as they watch the video.

Discussion (15 minutes):

- You can use the discussion questions below, use the reflection questions in each chapter, or come up with your own questions.
- As I mentioned, the material covered in the videos may bring up different emotions in your group participants, so be sensitive to this and adjust your discussion time as needed.
- Make sure to facilitate discussion where everyone feels safe to share and knows that any private information will not be shared outside the group. Also make sure the discussion is not dominated by one or two people.

Prayer (5 minutes):

- I recommend setting up pairs in your group as prayer partners during this study. You can either assign a prayer partner for the entire study or have participants pair up at the end of each study. I have found this helps individuals feel safe to voice their personal prayer requests, be heard, and receive the prayer they need.
- You may also want to close in a group prayer as well.

If you have more than one hour, you can extend the discussion and prayer time.

Discussion Questions

Introduction

Consider facilitating introductions this first week before the video. Ask group members to share their names and one detail about themselves. Depending on the size of your group, this may end up taking the place of your discussion after the video.

The gospel message is shared in the Introduction video, so you may want to have follow-up materials prepared for those who commit their lives or make a recommitment to Christ.

This week's memory verse is Isaiah 61:1:

> *The Spirit of the Sovereign Lord is on me,*
> *because the Lord has anointed me*
> *to proclaim good news to the poor.*
> *He has sent me to bind up the brokenhearted,*
> *to proclaim freedom for the captives*
> *and release from darkness for the prisoners.*

Reflection Questions:

You may want to use the reflection questions in this chapter as discussion questions. Allow God to lead you in choosing which questions to use.

1. Do you see yourself as the broken pot in the story? If so, how?
2. Do you see others' brokenness and judge them based on their past mistakes?
3. What are some practical ways we can see ourselves and others as God sees us instead of seeing the brokenness?

Share with the group how there will be a memory verse each week and how they can apply it to their lives.

Here are several ways you can meditate on this week's memory verse:

1. Write out this week's verse on an index card and carry it with you.
2. Set up a daily reminder on your mobile device to review the verse.

3. Consider changing your screen saver to this week's verse.
4. Write the verse on your mirror with a dry erase marker.
5. Post the verse around your home with sticky notes.
6. Print off the Scripture cards and have them laminated. Download them here: www.brokencrayonsbook.com

Chapter One

This week's memory verse is 2 Corinthians 5:17:

> *Therefore, if anyone is in Christ, the new creation has come: The old has gone, the new is here!*

General Questions:

1. What impacted you the most from this week's reading and video?
2. What do you think it means to forgive someone from our hearts? What might that look like in our lives?
3. Have you known someone who has a hard time forgiving others? What effects did the bitterness and resentment seem to have on his or her life?

Reflection Questions:

You may want to use the reflection questions in this chapter as discussion questions. Allow God to lead you in choosing which questions to use.

1. Is there any unconfessed sin that you need to bring to God today?

   If something comes to mind, stop and confess it to God right now. (Consider allowing time for silent prayer or play soft music in the background.)

2. Is there someone who has deeply hurt you whom you need to forgive through the power of Christ?
   If so, ask for God's help to walk through the steps of forgiveness.

3. Are you weighed down with shame and regret from your past mistakes? What are the areas where you need to forgive yourself and truly accept Christ's forgiveness for your sins?

If there is something in particular that comes to mind, ask God to help you let go of the shame and regret and live instead in His righteousness now. (Consider allowing time for silent prayer or play soft music in the background.)

Chapter Two

This week's memory verse is Romans 8:38–39:

> *For I am convinced that neither death nor life, neither angels nor demons, neither the present nor the future, nor any powers, neither height nor depth, nor anything else in all creation, will be able to separate us from the love of God that is in Christ Jesus our Lord.*

General Questions:

1. This week's topic is a deep topic. We realize it may have brought up emotions that are difficult to share in a group setting. If you would like to talk to someone one-on-one, let us know.
2. What impacted you the most from this week's reading and video?
3. Sexual strongholds are not talked about much in the church. Why do you think that is? What can we do to talk about sexuality in a healthy, biblical way?

Reflection Questions:

You may want to use the reflection questions in this chapter as discussion questions. Allow God to lead you in choosing which questions to use. If you use these questions in a group, you may want to consider allowing time for silent prayer or play soft music in the background.

1. What stuck out to you from Shelley's story in this chapter and video? How did it stir emotions within you?
2. Are there any wounds from your past that need healing? If so, are you ready and willing to begin the healing process with the help of God?
3. Is there anyone you need to forgive from your past?
4. Jesus is the only one able to bring healing to your broken heart. What does that statement mean to you? Do you believe it to be true for yourself?

5. What is God saying to you today regarding your own wounds from the past?

Chapter Three

This week's memory verse is Psalm 139:14:

> *I praise you because I am fearfully and wonderfully made;*
> *your works are wonderful,*
> *I know that full well.*

General Questions:

1. What impacted you the most from this week's reading and video?
2. Do you think body image issues are an issue in our culture today? Why or why not?
3. In what ways do you think the media is impacting us the most in this area of body image?

Reflection Questions:

You may want to use the reflection questions in this chapter as discussion questions. Allow God to lead you in choosing which questions to use.

1. What has been your biggest struggle related to body image?
2. Have you tried to compensate for the flaws you see in yourself? If so, how?
3. Do you believe this truth today: "My value comes from God, my Creator, and not from my appearance and what others think of me"? What do you think is holding you back from fully embracing who you are in Christ?
4. Have different group members write these phrases on sticky notes and put them up on the wall. Ask them which phrase speaks to them the most right now.

   I am accepted (Ephesians 1:6)
   I am cherished (Ephesians 5:29)
   I am chosen (1 Peter 2:9)
   I am complete in Christ (Colossians 2:10)
   I am created in His image (Genesis 1:27)
   I am forgiven (1 John 1:9)

I am cared for (1 Peter 5:7)
I am precious (Isaiah 43:4)
I am a new creation (2 Corinthians 5:17)
I am pleasing to God (Psalm 149:4)
I am protected (Psalm 91:14)
I am set free (John 8:32)
I live in victory (1 Corinthians 15:57)
I am treasured (Psalm 83:3)
I am valuable (Luke 12:24)

Chapter Four

This week's memory verse is Matthew 5:16:

> *In the same way, let your light shine before others, that they may see your good deeds and glorify your Father in heaven.*

General Questions:

1. What impacted you the most from this week's reading and video?
2. Rejection is something everyone faces at some time in his or her life. Let's list different forms of rejection (start a list on the board or a piece of paper: e.g., divorce, a breakup, not getting a job promotion, etc.).
3. Think of a time when something embarrassing happened to you. Can you identify how your belief filter changed after that experience, if at all?

Reflection Questions:

You may want to use the reflection questions in this chapter as discussion questions. Allow God to lead you in choosing which questions to use.

1. What gifts has God given you?
2. Have you ever hidden your gifts due to fear of rejection or failure?
3. In what ways have you faced rejection, big or small?
4. What is one thing you can do to come out of the shadows and let the light of Christ shine through you today?

Chapter Five

This week's memory verse is Isaiah 55:8–9:

> *"For my thoughts are not your thoughts,*
> *neither are your ways my ways,"*
> *declares the Lord.*
> *"As the heavens are higher than the earth,*
> *so are my ways higher than your ways*
> *and my thoughts than your thoughts."*

General Questions:

1. What impacted you the most from this week's reading and video?
2. There are so many things that happen that are difficult to understand this side of heaven. Why do you think we as humans want to know the answer to the question "why"?
3. Shelley mentioned in the video that God not only has all our puzzle pieces, but He also has the box top. What do you think this means and was this helpful to you?

Reflection Questions:

You may want to use the reflection questions in this chapter as discussion questions. Allow God to lead you in choosing which questions to use.

1. Has your family been through something tragic that changed your life? Your experience might be completely different from Shelley's, but any tragedy can be life altering.
2. What do you tend to rely on during times of crisis? Do you try to survive on your own strength, or do you trust God to get you through?
3. Emotions are God's gift to us. The author of Ecclesiastes wrote that "there is a time for everything, and a season for every activity under the heavens" (3:1). The point is that while it might not be any fun to experience conflicting emotions, it is okay to cry, to hurt, and to grieve. However, it is important to not let your emotions control you. Have you ever felt like it was not okay to show emotion? When and/or why?
4. What do you sense God telling you today?

Chapter Six

This week's memory verse is Psalm 23:5:

> *You prepare a table before me*
> *in the presence of my enemies.*
> *You anoint my head with oil;*
> *my cup overflows.*

General Questions:

1. What impacted you the most from this week's reading and video?
2. As we close this book study, what do you think God has taught you through these lessons? Was it helpful for you?
3. What do you think are your next steps?

Reflection Questions:

You may want to use the reflection questions in this chapter as discussion questions. Allow God to lead you in choosing which questions to use.

1. Do you relate at all to Shelley's broken cup story? If so, how?
2. In what ways have you seen others try to satisfy themselves apart from God? How have you done this?
3. Are you willing and ready to start a lifelong journey of finding your satisfaction in Christ alone? If so, how?
4. What, if anything, is standing in your way? What will you do to overcome the obstacles you have identified as standing in your way?

Notes

1. "The Cracked Pot," Bible.org, published July 20, 2009, accessed August 1, 2016 https://bible.org/illustration/cracked-pot.

2. John Eldredge, *Wild at Heart: Discovering the Secret of a Man's Soul*, (Nashville: Thomas Nelson, 2005), 127–28.

3. Goodreads.com, accessed September 1, 2016, https://www.goodreads.com/quotes/1025624-a-smile-is-the-best-makeup-a-girl-could-wear.

4. "G622 – apollymi – Strong's Greek Lexicon (KJV)," Blue Letter Bible, accessed September 8, 2016, https://www.blueletterbible.org/lang/lexicon/lexicon.cfm?Strongs=G622&t=KJV

5. "G2989 – lampō – Strong's Greek Lexicon (KJV)," Blue Letter Bible, accessed September 8, 2016, https://www.blueletterbible.org/lang/lexicon/lexicon.cfm?Strongs=G2989&t=KJV.

6. "G2041 – ergon – Strong's Greek Lexicon (KJV)," Blue Letter Bible, accessed September 8, 2016, https://www.blueletterbible.org/lang/lexicon/lexicon.cfm?Strongs=G2041&t=KJV.

7. Ibid.

8. Corrie ten Boom, *The Hiding Place*, 35th Anniversary Edition (Grand Rapids, MI: Chosen Books, 2006), 12.

9. *The Quotable Oswald Chambers*, David McCasland, ed. (Grand Rapids, MI: Discovery House, 2008), 155.

10. Hyrum W. Smith, *You Are What You Believe: Simple Steps to Transform Your Life* (Oakland, CA: Berrett-Koehler, 2016), 80.

11. Larry Crabb, *Connecting: Healing Ourselves and Our Relationships* (Nashville: Thomas Nelson, 2005), 32.

Made in United States
North Haven, CT
04 October 2023

42350820R00065